TO: Owen (1)

FROM: Owen (myself)

ART DIRECTION: Trinidad Vergara
DESIGN: Raquel Cané
Paintings by Emilio Pettoruti

© 2005 V & R Editoras / V & R Publishers

www.vergarariba.com

ISBN 987-9338-65-0

Printed in Singapore

FOR A SUCCESSFUL
MAN

Edited by Lidia María Riba

Leaders and Winners

In the simplest terms, a leader
is one who knows where he wants to go,
gets up, and goes.

JOHN ERSKINE

The question: *"Who ought to be the boss?"* is like saying *"Who ought to be the tenor in the quartet?"* Obviously, the man who can sing tenor.

HENRY FORD

We are not interested in the possibilities of defeat.

QUEEN VICTORIA

All men of action are dreamers.

JAMES E. HUNEKER

The man who is certain to advance
is the one who is too big for his place.

WALLACE D. WATTLES

The first and best victory is to conquer oneself.

PLATO

The ability
to accept responsibility
is the measure of the man.

ROY L. SMITH

Leadership is the ability
to get men to do
what they don't want to do
and like doing it.

HARRY TRUMAN

A wise man will make
more opportunities than he finds.

FRANCIS BACON

Whoever employs you does so
for a selfish motive.
You must be worth more to him
than the money he pays you.

David Seabury

A good manager is one
who isn't worried about his own career but rather
the careers of those who work for him.

H.S.M. Burns

11

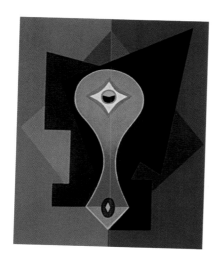

Try not to become
a man of success but rather
try to become a man of value.

ALBERT EINSTEIN

Many a man owes his success to his first wife
and his second wife to his success.

RED BUTTONS

12

I do not try to dance better than anyone else.
I only try to dance better than myself.

MIKHAIL BARYSHNIKOV

When I'm on my game, I don't think
there's anybody that acan stop me.

MICHAEL JORDAN

Becoming number one is easier
than remaining number one.

BILL BRADLEY

The Road Taken

You see things,

and you say, *"Why?"*

But I dream things that never were,

and I say, *"Why not?"*

GEORGE BERNARD SHAW

Everyone is going to the shore of attainment.
If you attempt the supreme goal,
all lesser goals are achieved.
Because I am moving along the spiritual path,
all lesser goals will be fulfilled.
All my aspirations will be met.

JOHN McLOUGHLIN

All my life people have said
I wasn't going to make it.

TED TURNER

16

I saw under the sun that the race is not won
by the swift, nor the battle by the valiant.

ECCLESIASTES

Either do not attempt at all
or go through with it.

OVID

There is always room at the top.

DANIEL WEBSTER

Give wind and tide a chance to change.

RICHARD E. BYRD

The thought, the dream, the vision,
always precede the act.

ORISON SWETT MARDEN

It is never too late to be
what you might have been.

GEORGE ELIOT

We are creators, and we can form today the world
we personally shall be living in tomorrow.

ROBERT COLLIER

If we are intended for great ends,
we are called to great hazards.

CARDINAL NEWMAN

Every disadvantage has an equivalent advantage
– if you'll take the trouble to find it.

W. CLEMENT STONE

Do not suppose opportunity
will knock twice at your door.

NICOLAS DE CHAMFORT

There's a way to do it better – find it.

THOMAS A. EDISON

If I have faith that I can do something,
I will surely acquire the capacity to do it,
even if I did not have it when I began.

MAHATMA GANDHI

We will either find a way, or we will build it.

HANNIBAL

If you want to reach the highest,
start from the lowest.

PUBLIUS SYRUS

To accomplish great things,
we must dream as well as act.

ANATOLE FRANCE

Success is not the result of spontaneous combustion. You must set yourself on fire.

Reggie Leach

You are never given a wish
without also being given
the power to make it true.

Richard Bach

A rock pile ceases to be a rock pile the moment
a single man contemplates it, bearing within him
the image of a cathedral.

ANTOINE DE SAINT-EXUPÉRY

It's easy to have faith in yourself and have discipline
when you're a winner, when you're number one.
What you've got to have is faith and discipline
when you're not a winner.

VINCE LOMBARDI

Secrets of Success

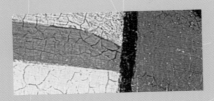

Winning isn't everything,
but wanting to win is.

VINCE LOMBARDI

I do the best I know how,
the very best I can; and I mean
to keep on doing so until the end.

ABRAHAM LINCOLN

The secret of success lies not
in doing your own work,
but recognizing the right man
to do it.

ANDREW CARNEGIE

Mere money-making
has never been my goal.
I had an ambition to build.

JOHN D. ROCKEFELLER

Even the woodpecker owes his success
to the fact that he uses his head
and keeps pecking away until he finishes
the job he starts.

COLEMAN COX

Success is the child of audacity.

BENJAMIN DISRAELI

Success... seems to be
connected with action.
Successful men keep moving.
They make mistakes, but they don't quit.

CONRAD HILTON

Do one thing extremely well,
then move on to the next thing.

PETER N. ZARLENGA

If A is success in life,
then A equals X plus Y plus Z.
Work is X; Y is play; and Z
is keeping your mouth shut.

ALBERT EINSTEIN

A man is never master of an idea
until he can express it clearly.
LEW SARETT

What this power is I cannot say; all I know is
that it exists and it becomes available only
when a man is in that state of mind
in which he knows exactly what he wants
and is fully determined not to quit until he finds it.

ALEXANDER GRAHAM BELL

No one can possibly achieve
any real and lasting success or get rich in business
by being a conformist.

J. PAUL GETTY

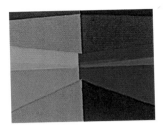

The secret of business is to know something
that nobody else knows.

ARISTOTLE ONASSIS

The first step in getting anywhere
is deciding that you are not going to stay
where you are.

J. P. MORGAN

If you never try you can never succeed — if you try
and do the best you can, you will never fail.

JIM RODGERS

To win, you must have the talent and desire
— but desire is first.

Sam Snead

The heights by great men reached and kept
Were not attained by sudden flight,
But they, while their companions slept,
Were toiling upward in the night.

Henry Wadsworth Longfellow

To play great music,
you must keep your eyes
on a distant star.

YEHUDI MENUHIN

I'm a firm believer
that people only do their best
at things they truly enjoy.

JACK NICKLAUS

An idea can turn to dust or magic
depending on the talent
that rubs against it.

WILLIAM BERNBACH

The road to success becomes lonely
because most are not willing
to face and conquer the hardships
that lurk on that road.
The ability to take that extra step
when you are tired is the quality
that separates the winners from the rest.

EDWARD LE BARON, JR.

Start by doing what is necessary, then what is possible
and suddenly, you are doing the impossible.

J. P. MORGAN

You never work for someone else.
The truth is someone is paying you
to work for yourself.

PAUL J. MEYER

Your success depends on the success
of the people around you.

BENJAMIN H. BRISTOL

Help people become
more motivated
by guiding them to the source
of their own power.

PAUL G. THOMAS

The trouble with success
is that it immediately diminishes
your mental conception
of what it should be.

TOM STOPPARD

When you get right down to the root
of the meaning of the word "succeed",
you find that it simply means to follow through.

F. W. NICHOL

Success is not so much
achievement as achieving.
Refuse to join the cautious crowd
that plays not to lose; play to win.

DAVID J. MAHONEY

Success consists in the climb.

ELBERT HUBBARD

Inner Success

Success has always been easy to measure.
It is the distance between one's origins
and one's final achievement.

MICHAEL KORDA

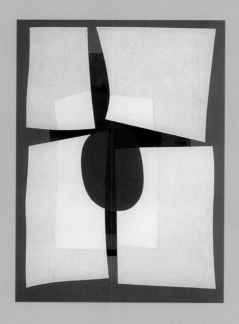

The common idea that success
spoils people by making them vain,
egotistic and complacent is erroneous
– on the contrary it makes them,
for the most part, humble, tolerant and kind.
Failure makes people bitter and cruel.

W. SOMERSET MAUGHAM

A man is a success if he gets up
in the morning and goes to bed at night
and in between does what he wants to do.

BOB DYLAN

The best part of one's life
is the working part. Believe me, I love to succeed...
However, the real spiritual
and emotional excitement is in the doing.

GARSON KANIN

Every winner has scars.

HERBERT N. CASSON

Our greatest glory is not in never failing,
but in rising every time we fall.

CONFUCIUS

If a man loves the labour
of his trade, apart from
any questions of success or fame,
the gods have called him.

ROBERT LOUIS STEVENSON

If we do our best we are a success.

WYNN DAVIS

When you reach the top...

Take some time to enjoy:
    The road has been long and hard.
Take some time to help others:
    Much has been given to you.
Take some time to share your triumph:
    Those who love you also climbed by your side.
Take some time to look back to where you started from:
    You will judge yourself less severely.
Take some time to rest a little:
    There is a new summit to conquer.

L. M. R.